SEX POSITIVE

SEX POSITIVE

A Gay Contribution To Sexual And Spiritual Union

by Larry J. Uhrig

Boston · Alyson Publications, Inc.

Special thanks must be given to Alan Fox for his faithful work on this manuscript and his labor of love in uniting my handwriting with his word processor.

A special word of thanks to my friend and colleague Don Eastman for his critical comments and valued suggestions.

This is a paperback original from Alyson Publications, Inc.,
40 Plympton St., Boston, Mass. 02118.
Distributed in Great Britain by GMP Publishers,
PO Box 247, London, N16 6RW.

ISBN 0-932870-82-1

First Edition

First Printing: June 1986

Contents

*To the blessed memories of every
gay and lesbian person who died in the closet
and to the one man who truly opened the door
to liberty and life.*

*To Troy D. Perry,
who opened the door of the church.*

Introduction

The enlightenment of the human spirit can be enriched in many different ways – certainly, books are high on the list and this one is filled with enlightenment for everyone who reads it. Rev. Uhrig is bold to claim that "homosexuality plays a prophetic role in uniting spirituality and sexuality for all people." He makes a very convincing case in support of that claim and from our personal experience we know hundreds of others who would agree.

In simple, artful phrases, this book reveals the sex negativity of Judeo-Christian culture as the major obstacle in spiritualizing our sexuality. Rev. Uhrig further believes, at least he hints at it, that our sexuality may well be the doorway to a new dimension of mystical communication and the Divine.

What a refreshing way to look at what for most of us has caused shame and guilt in the past – to reorganize our thinking about it and to discover that it provides a new way to be open to prayer and a spiritual life built on something as intensely personal and unavoidable as our sexuality.

Without attempting to rehash all the old arguments about Scriptural condemnation of homosexuality, this book offers new insights far more profound than they first appear. It is as if Rev. Uhrig wants to begin the development of a new theology of sexuality, incorporating the experience and insights of spiritually enlightened gay women and men.

This work will stir controversy, especially from the more rigid fundamentalists and traditionalists. The work of scriptural exegesis will continue until the end of time. However, it is truths and insights such as those expounded in this small volume, that continue to validate the interpretation of revelation.

The proposals offered for the growth of a new sexual ethic, rising from the gay experience, will truly be recognized by those of us who share it, and hopefully spread to the entire Christian community by those of us who care. Read this book more than once. It contains the seeds of a new, enlightened theology that makes our sexuality a core feature of our spirituality. It seems to us that the Holy Spirit is overseeing this work.

Andrew Mattison, Ph.D.
David McWhirter, M.D.
Authors of *The Male Couple*
San Diego, California

Preface

We live in a sex negative world. We have been raised in sex negative value systems and religions. For too many years gay and lesbian people have spoken in apologetic ways seeking to change the hearts and minds of others. Our passive address has been ignored by many. Attempts to show a new view of religion and sexuality have been largely unsuccessful. We can no longer sit quietly by while other spokespersons for religion continue to preach from ignorance and fear. We must speak out boldly a new message. We must be prophets of a sex positive truth.

For years I joined the attempt to persuade. I debated all the religious issues and the Biblical quotations. What resulted was no measurable change in anyone's mind. An incident occurred in the fall of 1984 on a television show. The host said something which was simply not true. My response was to interrupt him. I said, "This is not true." The abrupt and unexpected challenge stopped the conversation. I was able to insert the correct information. The host of the show simply said, "Oh, that changes the whole issue," and we dropped the subject. Then and there I realized that people did not expect gay people to challenge old ideas with any kind of self-confidence or authority.

Changing sex negative attitudes requires an aggressive presentation of a positive message. We must be willing to say things like: "That's not true," "That's a lie," and "That is ignorant." We do begin to change the world when we witness to our truth rather than argue over someone else's ideology. What I have done in *Sex Positive* is to state a new view of truth. I have set out in a new direction which leaves behind old and unuseful concepts of God, Scripture, sexuality, and spirituality. We must depart from the old and enter into a new era of thinking and knowing. Gay and lesbian prophets are speaking a new vision. This vision and its truth will reform the old structures of human relationship and give new meaning and life to the family, the church, and society.

We can no longer waste countless pages debating what the Bible does or does not say. The issue has been settled by more than a couple dozen competent scholars and theologians. It is time to move beyond debate to make our contribution to the union of the worlds of sexuality and spirituality. Gay people have been raised up by God in this age to be a source of human healing and a place of divine revelation. Let the world welcome our message as one which brings hope. Let the church give thanks for our faithfulness and make room for our gifts. There is a sex positive message. The door is open and will never be shut. I invite the reader to walk through this open door. I invite you to challenge your traditions. I ask you to join me in speaking truth.

Larry J. Uhrig
Washington, DC

1

Sex Negative

The issue is sexuality. It lies at the heart of the human rights struggle of women and gay people in America in the 1980s and 1990s. The ordination of women and gays in our churches, the civil rights agendas in counties, states, and the nation, jobs and housing for sexual minorities, are all issues of sexuality.

If we are to move beyond the present, a time characterized by significant barriers to healthy, social adjustment, then we must assault the structures that inhibit growth and prevent the average youth from growing to wholeness. This means setting an agenda that shall unite sexuality and spirituality. This union will help us as a society to bless human relationships, achieve stable pair bonding, and create responsible legal instruments that protect and nurture life.

Our task is to rethink the role of sexuality in our culture and to expose the social and religious taboos that undergird our value system. We must rethink our interpretation of the basic symbols of our culture. We must reform the institutions that have been used to hold our sexuality and spirituality in tension. We must speak the prophetic message emerging out of gay and lesbian spirituality. This message will lead the religious institutions of our culture back to faithfulness to their basic tenets.

This defined assault upon the symbol structure of our culture should not be a threat to us, but rather a welcomed and long overdue gift. This gift can release us from bondage to fear and ignorance. Our new openness to sexuality and pursuit of spirituality will help create healthy family structures and build relationships based in honesty and trust.

Sex Positive means the integration of our sexuality with all the other components of our life and personal identities. It means exploring our sexuality and its spiritual base, our spirituality and its sexual components.

Social Taboos

For generations gay people have lived in secret — a veiled existence characterized by secret codes and an underground lifestyle. The lives of homosexual people had been largely defined by fear. For most of our society, to be gay meant to be sexual. Sexuality evokes fear in us. We have reacted to this fear by seeking to deny sexuality.

Sexuality is a dominant and pervasive force in life and yet we seek to control it and submerge it beneath the surface of life.

Growing up in Western culture means having to explore sexuality without clear direction. For me it meant picking up bits and pieces on the school bus.

The emerging picture was fragmented with no clear focus. The growing and explosive stuff inside was not met with objective and rational teaching. The parenting generation gave instruction to the children: "Don't touch that part of your body. . ." (meaning our genitals). We learned nicknames for our genitals rather than the biological or clinical terms. Life was a process of covering up, of hiding. We lived in the conflict of hiding our "private parts" while seeking to know truth, growth, and maturity.

This hide-and-seek continues to fracture our lives and foster guilt about those intimate realities of our nature, realities of sex, orgasm, and sexual relationships with others.

Each of us was left to our own devices in seeking the truth, seeking experience, seeking release of sexual tension and answers to questions. Unlocking the mystery of sexuality was not met with social approval or social instruments and structures to aid the process. Our seeking and questioning was often met with silence and evasion.

I remember the cloaked whispers of parents when discussing the fact that an unmarried woman acquaintance was pregnant. Sexuality outside of marriage was *anathema*. It was not to be discussed openly. Then there were the allusions to homosexuality, references to men who were 'funny, queer, fruits,' and other terms to hide to the realities of same sex love, attraction, and relationship.

We were taught that sexuality and the attendant emotions were private matters. To display any form of them in public, except in defined, specifically acceptable ways, was condemned, a breach of social etiquette.

Growing up without a forum to question or channels to explore one's emerging sexual identity has inhibited and debilitated the health and maturation process of all people. To consider the plight of those of us growing up gay meant to add on layer after layer of guilt and obstacles to healthy social adjustment.

Sex has been cast in a negative light. Sure, it was a part of life, but a part to be strictly contained. It is the process of containment and restriction that must be examined and understood if we are to break the pattern of negativity and move toward a positive and joyful understanding of sex. The goal is to create a climate of gratitude in which sex and sexuality find true expression.

Achievement of this goal is fraught with conflict. On the surface it appears that sex is an open subject in our society. Sex is everywhere. We use it to sell products and promote commercial ventures. Sex is the force beneath so much of our communication and relationships, yet we deny its importance and seek to keep it contained. The contradiction is clear: sex, while useful to achieve our commercial goals, is denied and banished from overt exploration. We seem unable, as a culture, to allow sex to take a normal place within our lives and relationships. We must find balance.

Like a surging force inside, sexuality seeks its own expression in word, thought, and deed. This seeking in the environment of hiding produces neurotic behavior, fears, and destructive guilt. All of this is unnecessary.

We have a structure of social taboos with regard to sexuality, supported by religious systems and value judgments designed to maintain a straitjacket effect. This straitjacket contains and restricts movement.

The Religious Taboos

The social taboos could not survive if it were not for a religious value system which fuels the process of the containment and restriction of sexuality. This system operates to maintain a distinct separation of sexuality and spirituality. Spirituality and religion are often defined with an absence of references to sexual and physical things. Indeed, intense states of spirituality are often defined as an absence of physical reality and specifically of sexuality. Intense experience of sexuality, on the other hand, is characterized as the absence of spirituality and often the opposite of spirituality. These two essential components of human nature and relationships are cast as enemies of one another. Our task is to uncover this lie and gross distortion of reality for the purpose of uniting these two compatible realities once again. To achieve this task, let us look at the following components of religious taboos:

1. a history of Biblical Ignorance

2. answering the question "What is natural?"

3. seeking to find sexual ethics where only procreation ethics exist

4. The institution of marriage.

A History of Biblical Ignorance

Questioning the relationship between sexuality and spirituality necessitates a confrontation with Scripture. Scripture is both the source of much spiritual nurture and truth while also being the locus of much misunderstanding with regard to sexuality. It must be said boldly and simply: A knowledgeable and scholarly study of the Bible reveals three important facts:

1. The Bible does not discuss or reveal any knowledge of homosexuality as sexual identity or orientation.

2. Every Biblical reference to homosexual acts is found in a context of discussions of idol worship and/or abusive behavior.

3. Some textual problems and translation questions seem ambiguous and unclear as to the original meaning.

Texts which are generally used to support a condemnation of homosexuality are consistently misused. The following texts form the body of the Biblical material which has been used against gay people. These texts are:

Genesis 19
Deuteronomy 23:17-18
Leviticus 18:22
I Corinthians 6:9
I Timothy 1:10
Romans 1:26-27
The Creation Accounts in Genesis 1 and 2

These texts have been analyzed and presented in many books published in the past ten years or more. It is not my intention to restate here material so readily available elsewhere. I will, however, recommend the books listed in the appendix as important resources for study.

My point is simple. When the Scripture is taken seriously, the result is that one cannot substantiate a condemnation of homosexuality. To take the Scripture seriously requires that the reader give attention to questions of inspiration, critical interpretation, textual criticism, historical criticism, source criticism, and form criticism. To neglect these tools of classical Biblical criticism is to withhold from Scripture the serious and faithful treatment deserved.

Any approach to Scripture must answer the question of who was writing to whom and for what purpose. To understand the meaning of a text one must first discover the original situation the text addresses.

The tragedy of our current era is that a vocal religious right-wing movement has swayed the hearts and minds of millions of people. It is ironic that those who seek to base their political and social doctrine upon Scriptural truth should themselves distort and pervert the text of the Bible.

A classic example of proof texting and distorting the text from its context occurs in many traditional marriage ceremonies. Often the bride and groom will say to one another, "Entreat me not to leave you or to return from following you; for where you go I will go, and where you lodge I will lodge; your people shall be my people, and your God my God; where you die I will die, and there will I be buried." (Ruth 1:16-17, RSV). These words, so often shared between a man and a woman, are part of a covenant made between two women. This context is conveniently overlooked to serve heterosexual cultural values. While it is certainly acceptable to use the meaning of these words, it is important to acknowledge the original context.

Perhaps the most explicit covenant of relationship and love found anywhere in Scripture is the one made between David and Jonathan. The covenant and history of the love between David and Jonathan is recorded in the books of I Samuel and II Samuel. This record is one of love, commitment, and intimacy. It is strange that the two major relationship covenants within Scripture occur between same-sex couples. Much has already been written and said about the themes of sexuality which run throughout Scripture. It is the task of modern persons to allow those themes to emerge and find expression within the lives and community of people of faith. We shall return to these specific texts and other Biblical questions later in a discussion of the positive Biblical base for sexual/spiritual merger.

What Is Natural?

Two factors determine the answer to the question "What is natural?" These are a confused understanding of St. Paul's writing and a selective interpretation of the Genesis Creation accounts.

Let us first look at the Genesis accounts. Those who would make a case that homosexuality is against the natural order tend to ground their argument in an interpretation of Genesis Chapter 1. This account gives major attention to the command: "Be fruitful and multiply, and fill the earth and subdue it." (Genesis 1:28, RSV). This command certainly makes sense when understood as an address to a small tribe of people who are surrounded by enemies, whose survival is dependent upon biological growth.

Advocates of this interpretation of the purpose of creation and sex tend to ignore the creation account found in Chapter 2. The story in Chapter 2 is earlier, predating Chapter 1 by some 400 to 500 years. The emphasis of the second, older story is upon companionship and mutual support and nurture. In this context, sexuality is only one of the many components of a relationship.

Again, much has been written about what is natural. My thesis is simply that we have historically used our interpretation of Scripture to minimize sexuality, to advocate only a limited and restricted view of sexuality, i.e. heterosexuality, and to deny the rights of those who do not share this view. Such a one-sided, narrow interpretation of sexuality's role in human relationship does not serve to further healthy, mature pair bonding.

When St. Paul talks about what is natural, he is referring to that which conforms to Jewish law. If we are to subscribe to this interpretation, we must at least be willing to be consistent. Therefore, we must be willing to adhere to the whole law. It is inconsistent to seek to enforce a portion of the law such as the holiness codes of Leviticus with regard to sexual behavior while at the same time ignoring the rest of the law which addresses a multitude of human behavior, most notably diet and dress. Keeping the whole law requires that we pay attention to such things as diet, dress, and the many other proscriptions of human behavior.

We must understand that the law was designed to set the Jew apart from all other peoples, to make a distinct nation, visible and unique. The law succeeded historically in this function. When Paul speaks of being natural he is advocating the tenets of Orthodox Judaism. Again, we can see the danger of taking Biblical texts out of their historical context. To seek an interpretation of a Biblical text without the use of the critical tools referred to above is to grossly distort the true meaning and purpose of the text in question, thereby missing both the point and power of the text.

Seeking a Sexual Ethic

A critical issue which must be addressed if we are to discover the true place of sexuality in our lives is to answer the question "What are our sexual ethics?" Very simply put: we lack any specific sexual ethics. The Church has offered our society not a sexual ethic but rather a procreation ethic. Sex for procreation is but one function of sex and certainly not the major function. The human sexual act is engaged in for purposes of pleasure, love, and intimate communication far more frequently than it is for the purpose of procreation. We have inherited a procreation ethic which presents itself as a sexual ethic.

As discussed above, a single-minded and narrow

focus upon the Genesis 1 creation narrative forms the moral and Biblical supports for a procreation ethic. Sex is understood only as serving the procreation function. This selective interpretation of the creation stories has remained with us to this day. We have tailored a "sexual ethic" to fit the social and religious needs of our society. In doing this we have attempted to lock sex into the structure of heterosexual marriage. We have valued the procreation aspects of human sexual behavior and devalued the recreational aspects. The process serves the purpose of containing and restraining sex in order to manage our fears.

Observation of our present sexual behavior offers immediate evidence that sex is shared widely outside of the old forms of legal marriage. Any attempt to contain sex in the bonds of the institution of marriage has become a vain attempt to ignore reality and bridle sexuality.

An age in which it is possible to have sex without babies and babies without sex requires an ethic of sexuality which acknowledges wide human diversity. To create this ethic we must achieve a release of the social and religious restrictions on sexuality. There must be a permissiveness if there is to emerge a healthy balance in our sexual expression. If gay and lesbian people are to experience their sexual identities as healthy and good, we must help our culture to free itself from the bondage of procreation ethics. The place to begin is with the diversity of human sexuality. The increasing visibility of gay and lesbian people underscores the great need to find a sexual ethic which can be useful to all peoples.

The tragedy of our day is that religious leaders seek to shore up an old structure that is no longer capable of containing the diverse realities of our lives. Divorce rates, premarital and extramarital sex, and abortion are facts that clearly demonstrate how bankrupt our procreation-based sexual ethic really is.

The "new wine" of our experience cannot be contained in the old wineskin of the past. To pour new wine into old skins will burst them. A complete and responsible sexual ethic must allow for the traditional forms of sexual expression, but must also embrace the reality of gay, lesbian, bisexual, asexual, and transsexual persons.

Great quantities of energy have been channeled into efforts to contain sexuality. Procreation ethics are the result of this massive containment policy. Beneath this historic effort to restrict and contain human sexual expression lies a great fear. This fear has two sides, one being fear of sex itself and the other being the attempt to keep sexuality and spirituality separate.

There is a fracture running through ourselves, a chasm maintained to keep our sexual and spiritual selves apart from one another. The truth about this sexual/spiritual split is that these two dimensions of life are intertwined and interdependent rather than opponents of one another.

Thesis: Human sexual and spiritual energies lie at the nuclear center of our selfhood, informing one another. These two dimensions give each other energy and power. Therefore, it is essential for sexual/spiritual energies to merge rather than be held apart. Sexual energy without its spiritual base is random, dispersed, and destructive. Random sexual energy without its spiritual component loses power and meaning.

On the other hand, spiritual energy is sterile and impotent without the sexual component.

When human sexual energies are intense and frustrating to the point of distraction, one should look for an equally high level of spiritual energy. Giving spiritual energy a channel through which to flow gives form to random sexual energies. The opposite is also true, a heightened degree of spiritual life indicates an equally active sexuality. This needs to be recognized and addressed if we are to achieve healthy spiritual/ sexual selves.

Our culture and Western Judeo-Christian tradition have struggled for centuries to maintain a dualism intent upon keeping sex and spirit segregated. The procreation ethic has been a unfortunate product of this effort and the instrument for enforcing this ethic has been the institution of heterosexual marriage.

Marriage: A Moral Chastity Belt?

Let us recap. Procreation ethics are focused upon giving value to sex only for the purpose of procreation and devaluing the non-procreative intents of sex.

What is marriage? Before going further we must make a distinction between the legal/cultural function of marriage and the religious function. Here the term marriage refers only to the legal and contractual union between a man and a woman as defined by civil authorities. The spiritual union between two persons which seeks the recognition and blessing of the Church is a wholly separate entity. Such a spiritual relationship is appropriate between a man and a woman, two women, or two men and has no relationship to the restrictions of civil authorities. These two functions, the legal and the spiritual, should be kept distinct and separate. Therefore it is not the role of religious institutions to function on behalf of the civil authority.

The Rite of Blessing or Holy Union is appropriate only for persons of religious faith. These couples may seek such a blessing separately from the legal recognition of their union. Obviously gay or lesbian couples do not have affirmation by civil authorities available to them. If they are also persons who do not share a religious faith, they may experience difficulty in finding ways to affirm, celebrate, and symbolize their relationship.

Our society has offered only traditional marriage as the appropriate form to express sexual and spiritual union. Clearly this structure is not adequate for a great many people, especially gay people.

Before going further in this discussion of the institution of marriage, let me affirm that it is certainly possible for two heterosexual persons to find complete expression of love, sexuality, and spirituality within the forms of traditional marriage.

However, my observation and conviction is that marriage has been used for centuries as a chastity belt to contain, restrict, and control sexual expression. Not only has sex outside of marriage been devalued by church and society, but sex within marriage has been defined in the most restrictive ways. Even in the 1980s there are numerous laws that seek to restrict what is or is not proper behavior between a man and a woman. Worse than the laws are the guilt-laden attitudes which inhibit freedom of sexual response. While this is changing dramatically, we must realize that we are only now emerging from a sex negative past. This emergence is one of rebellion and rejection that needs sex positive guidance as well as freedom to seek a healthy balance in sexual expression.

Church and state alike have used the traditional structure of marriage as a shelter to avoid the real issues of sexuality, spirituality, and the situational choices confronting each person each moment.

Our society assumes that what is natural has already been defined. We have treated the Biblical questions about homosexuality as if they needed no further investigation. It should be obvious to all that with divorce rates at fifty percent and premarital and extramarital sexual expression normative, the attempt to force all people into the marriage formula has not worked. In fact, marriage with its conveniently defined roles has served to enslave the human spirit, denigrate women, and shut down the natural reciprocity between sex and spirit.

Marriage has become another part of property rights, a convenient way to assure transition between generations. The real casualty in this structure are the sincere men and women who seek to fit their unique selves into the roles and structures of traditional marriage.

The solution to this situation is not the abandonment of marriage but the renovation of marriage. This renovation will help restore individualism and honesty. It will also help unite sexuality and spirituality.

Both gay and non-gay couples seek to conform their relationships to values rooted in marriage. Example: Often couples talk about being "faithful" to one another. The word faithful is used to mean sexually exclusive. My point is that a relationship should not be defined by its sexual component. While sex is certainly important and a powerful presence, it should not be the defining factor. The attempt to define a relationship and the covenant in terms of sexual exclusivity is often rooted in fear. We are afraid of rejection, afraid that our spouse will find someone better. The root problem here is not sex but rather self-identity and self-esteem.

We need a new definition of faithfulness. Faithfulness means keeping the agreement or contract made. If the agreement involves an open sexual relationship – fine. If it defines a closed sexual relationship – fine. What is of utmost importance is the clarity of the agreement and that it be mutually shared. Two people are faithful if they keep their agreements. This requires deep levels of honesty and trust.

Here lies the challenge to traditional marriage. We have sought to create rules and regulations about relationships; we have sought to avoid the daily task of questioning. We have raised our children to fit themselves into the roles of husband and father, wife and mother. In doing so we have not given them the tools or relationship skills to address the diversity of human relationship or the complexity of their own sexual selves.

The call for honesty, trust, and a new sense of the meaning of faithfulness opens the door for the restoration of all relationships. Relationship models for the future must embrace the diversity of human experience. This position of openness offers health and good news for all relationships. People who desire traditional, heterosexual, sexually exclusive relationships can have them as a matter of choice, not as a response to a legislated morality. We should be free to make this traditional choice because we want it, not because it is considered "better" or "right" or "moral." Likewise, we must be freed to explore our sexuality and the modes of its expression.

Our goal is to produce a new and vital sense of ourselves and embrace our sexual/spiritual energies, in ways that result in good health.

A new openness that focuses upon building honesty and trust, and that questions the process of relationship formation, will help free many people from the traps of traditional marriage. Many gay and nongay men and women have entered into marriage because it was the "thing to do," expected of them, and a way to channel the volatile sexual energies which young people experience. This channel has become a straitjacket to control and restrict. Ultimately, people have broken out to freedom in order to find their true selves and to understand the complex dimensions of sexuality and spirituality.

If the open exploration of sexuality were nurtured rather than barricaded by social and religious taboos, more young people would enter marriage only after serious exploration of their motives. Traditional heterosexual marriage could become a more successful institution if it were enabled to be a contractual agreement between two persons based upon honesty and trust. Rather, it has become a rigid structure forged by church and state to bridle sexuality, and subdue fear. Fears about sexuality and the result of sexual/spiritual union can only be addressed by heading into them directly. Any attempt to camouflage or mask these fears results in granting them a disproportionate power over our lives. This power corrupts and distorts both sex and relationship. A direct address of sexual realities restores to health and wholeness our sexual selves and puts an end to the destructive influences of fear.

How shall we become free of the sex negative influence of our culture? How shall we find any objectivity which allows us to speak to the inadequacies of traditional heterosexual structures?

The answer is: By stepping out of these structures. Gay people offer a new vantage point, from which we may gain needed insight into the sexual/spiritual dilemmas which threaten to undo the fabric of Western culture.

Thesis: The experience of homosexual men and women in America since 1969 provides the key to answering the above question. Through our history of rebellion and disenfranchisement from the mainstream of American life, we have forged the key to a new kingdom, a commonwealth of equality and sexual/spiritual wholeness. It is in the gay and lesbian communities that heterosexuals will find the clues to freedom.

Moreover, it is from the gay Christian movement that religious persons will find the solution to the problem of saving relationships, uniting sexuality and spirituality and understanding Biblical truth.

The gay Christian witness is the place of revelation. What follows is a three-fold process of discovery through which we may come to an initial understanding of how the gay and lesbian experience plays the significant role of liberating hetero-religious bondage.

We begin with an examination of the homosexual journey from guilt and fear through rebellion to balance.

Next we will explore the components of a sex-positive ethic which provides a solid Biblical base for the homosexual experience. Once a sex positive interpretation of Scripture, sexuality, and relationship has been established, we can look at a case history of sexual/spiritual union. The key to this entire process is the claim that homosexuality plays a prophetic role in uniting sexuality with spirituality for all people. The freedom and balance needed in heterosexual relationships will be aided by the gifts and insight born in the gay experience.

2

The Homosexual Experience

For me, growing up gay meant seeking maturity in the context of anticipating rejection. It meant forming relationships in an atmosphere of guilt and shame. I felt like a mushroom forced to grow in a dark cellar.

For myself and millions of other homosexual children life was lived on many levels. Great quantities of energy were required to keep the various levels of life separate. Beneath the public world of school, play, and family relationships there was the secret world of emerging sexuality, and within that, the private sanctuary of sexual orientation.

The realities of the world I knew never encouraged discussion of sexuality itself much less my private secret.

Countless numbers of gay people grew up believing that they were the only gay person in the world. What was worse for many of us was that we didn't have a vocabulary to name our feelings or emerging identity. All we knew was that we were different from people around us and that this difference was not good.

Life was characterized by great amounts of guilt. "I was not normal" – so I thought. Somehow my condition was my own fault. I must have done something wrong. I was being punished. The worst part of guilt is not finding absolution. There was no place to discuss these feelings nor to find acceptance. Hiding the core of one's life is a difficult task, requiring great amounts of energy. Elaborate systems are created to manage guilt and reduce the abiding sense of shame that begins to pervade life. These systems of denial slowly destroy a person's self esteem.

The young gay person gets a consistent message from society that gay is not good. Schoolmates painfully reinforce this message by calling people "queer" or "fag." While this oppressive behavior is common knowledge to today's culture, we have yet to measure the disastrous toll on human lives and self esteem resulting from such behavior. Even worse, we have no way of knowing how many young men and women took their lives because they could not handle the guilt and the fear of being discovered. Facing the suicide of friends and the many attempts of others leaves one angry and sick at heart.

Gay and lesbian people continue to live in an environment which is basically ignorant of sexuality and homosexuality. For many gay people the gay experience is one of loneliness. The loneliness is a product of self defense. It has been necessary for gay people to hide the truth about themselves. The process meant withdrawing from many of life's social interactions. Many of us learned to stay away from sports and other endeavors which sought to force us into sex roles which were not compatible with our identity. Gay men and women found escape through schoolwork, books, and the arts. Generations of gays escaping from social pressure through these vehicles of self-expression have resulted in a very creative, expressive and gifted gay community. This community today leads the way in the arts, service industries, and creative business. We had to take care of ourselves and create our own security. In the end our adaptation to oppression and reaction to life's stress and pain produced survival for many of us.

The price of our survival and aloneness has been high. We have had to live outside the mainstream of society. We made our own subculture, created our own society. Much as coal under pressure for long periods of time becomes a priceless gem, so gay people so long oppressed have become the source of glittering new levels of achievement in the arts and new industries of our society – yes, I certainly intend to suggest a prophetic and saving role we play to restore and rebuild not only our understanding of human sexuality but our social structures and our cities as well. Much of the story of urban gentrification has been one of gay people bringing renewal to the city's life.

When we discuss Sex Positive we will look at this important role for gay and lesbian people. Nevertheless, the pathway to freedom has not been an easy or simple one.

The sex negative climate in which gay people are forced to mature is clearly visible in the following true story. Brian and his lover of five years were seeking to achieve a healthy relationship while also seeking to fit into the expectations and defined roles our society offers.

Brian came to talk to me about a relationship problem. The situation was one of two gay men seeking to find a place for their love and relationship within the existing structure of a devout Catholic family. The specific incident was one in which Brian sought the counsel and support of his brother and sister-in-law. The relatives presented themselves to Brian and his lover as being caring and understanding. Their concern was that Brian and his friend not engage in sexual activity. It was fine for them to be good friends and roommates, but it was 'sinful' for them to have a sexual relationship. Up to this point the story sounded rather normal, one I had heard many times before. But what followed was appalling to my ears. Brian's brother and his wife sought to demonstrate their love and support by offering to join them in their attempt to live a celibate lifestyle. They offered to remain celibate themselves for a period of six months as a sign of support and encouragement.

Nothing I had heard in my years of counseling had so clearly demonstrated the nature of the sex negative mind-set generated by religion and culture. The story shows not only the sex negative mentality of the persons involved, but also demonstrates the control and restraint function of marriage. It appears obvious to me that Brian's brother and wife had serious problems with sexuality. The entire story is encrusted with guilt, denial, and sex negative attitudes which I could only call malignant. The two overwhelming realities within this incident are the response of the brother and the fact that Brian and his lover were even willing to go along with this plan. Fortunately, this was a short-lived venture as by the time that Brian had come to me he and his lover had abandoned this folly.

The path to freedom must lead each of us out of this land of fear and guilt. It must lead out of fear, through rebellion, to freedom, and then to balance. Let us look at the four stages of liberation essential for a person to achieve a sex positive lifestyle.

Out of Fear

Human life is destroyed by fear. It breaks the spirit and eventually breaks the body. Physical sickness is not unrelated to the guilt, shame, and fear which has pervaded our lives as gay people. Fear of being found out has resulted in elaborate systems of denial and evasion. To be discovered means often to lose jobs, family support, relationships, livelihoods, and even life for some.

It is essential that gay and lesbian people be delivered from fear if they are to live healthy lives. This requires openness at all levels of social/cultural interaction. The truth cannot be hidden, it must be both acknowledged and celebrated.

No amount of compromise and cover-up is worth the price if indeed fear and hiding inhibit life and health. Our experience as gay people has brought us to the breaking point. That is the point at which we are no longer willing to compromise, to hide, to lie, about who we are. The next stage is rebellion.

Rebellion

To rebel is to fight back. It is to reject the old ways of doing things, it is to cease cooperating with the oppressive structures given to us by the state, our family, and the church. These structures inhibit human growth and prevent health.

Rebel we did and we still do. Our political rebellion has been dated from the Stonewall riots in New York in 1969 when gay men refused to accept police harassment in a gay bar. They fought back and in doing so destroyed the stereotype of a passive, weak and fearful minority. The moment we refuse to accept oppression we are free.

A year prior to Stonewall another rebellion began, one of a vastly different nature. In October of 1968 a young Pentecostal clergyman named Troy Perry announced the formation of a church to minister to homosexuals. The beginning of the Metropolitan Community Church signaled an end to generations of Biblical and theological ignorance. Each one of us has had our own story of rebellion, of breaking away from strictly defined behavior patterns and scripts of expectation. Rebellion is a stage we must pass through if we are to be free.

Observation of the experience of hundreds of gay people has given me a new view of our rebellion. The elements of the experience are (1) Anger, (2) Intentional mixing of social codes and expectations, even to the point of violating our value system, and (3) Exaggeration of behavior patterns.

Anger is not a highly valued quality in our society and yet it can serve as a healthy and productive response to the world around us. When gay men and women rebel against years of oppression and self-denial, anger is inescapable. Anger can be expressed violently, disrupting families and traditional social structures. An example of such a situation is one in which the gay child selects an important traditional family event such as Thanksgiving or Christmas dinner as the setting to announce his or her sexual orientation. Another variation may be the surprise introduction of one's spouse into an environment which has not been prepared to receive such news. Anger brings with it a certain essential shock value.

Anger built up over longer periods of time may also express itself passively. An example of this passive expression is the case of the middle-aged parent and father who simply goes to work one morning and never returns home. Some days later he informs the family that he has moved away with his male lover of several years to start a new life.

Anger must be experienced. When it is not, it may be turned inward to destroy the self. Such is the case of the young Baptist minister from suburban Washington who shot himself when his homosexual identity was made public. The pain of the event will linger on for years in the lives of the parishioners and family members. They will no doubt feel guilt from having participated in the oppression of gay people.

No one knows how many teenage suicides are a

result of anger turned inward as young men and women choose not to face the coming out process with all its fears and threats of rejection.

A large part of the process of rebellion can be seen in the intentional mixing of social codes and expectations. This acting out continues to be evident in young gay people.

Very simply put, acting out is a variation of an "I'll show them" attitude. I can recall my own acting out while I was in graduate school. If people expected a gay man to be effeminate I went out of my way not to disappoint them. I would wear flamboyant clothes, let my hair grow long, and adopt the stereotypical rebellious behavior of the late 1960s. Having grown up in a family where jewelry was not commonly worn, I of course began to wear lots of chains and rings. When in a crowd I was certain to speak loudly so as to shock nearby "straights." I recall more than a few occasions when other gay males and I would exclaim such "camp" phrases as "Oh, Mary, look at her," loudly in public places such as department stores. What was important to us was to assault the standards of others; by deliberately mixing the images presented, we challenged the expectations of others. Our goal was to confuse others and cause them to acknowledge our presence. It was also an assertion of ourselves, an expression of anger towards a non-accepting society.

At times our mixing of roles and the underlying anger would be confused. This resulted in overstated behavior which sometimes violated one's own personal values and standards.

The best example of this mixture of "I'll show them" and anger is often seen in sexual acting out.

If gay people were "supposed to be" promiscuous sexually we would show them what promiscuity was. Elements of self-hatred and lack of acceptance that are so much a part of the coming out process produce destructive behavior. A simple example is one of seeking of sexual partners in public restrooms where the threat and danger of both arrest and physical violence are high. I recall an incident of a young gay male being jumped and beat up by four men in a YMCA in Columbus, Ohio, while attempting to pick up a "trick." The event reinforced an attitude of "you deserve to be beaten." This event created psychological scars that lasted for years.

Numerous gay people have sought to establish new personal records of how many sexual contacts they could make in one evening. Often this behavior is rooted in an attempt to live out the negative social stereotype as a part of our rebellion. At the same time guilt is increased when one's own standards of sexual behavior are violated.

The "acting out" stage often lasts a considerable length of time. When gay people have ceased to act out overt rebellion, non-conformist behavior may continue to be expressed sexually.

The stage following rebellion is freedom. This may sound like we have achieved our goal. Freedom suggests that we have arrived, yet I believe it to be a part of a process. It is an extreme of a pendulum swing, rather than a stopping place.

Freedom

Rebellion leads to freedom – an unrestrained behavior pattern in which anything goes. I am talking about a stage gay people pass through in dealing with sexuality and sexual identity.

Coming out of the guilt and shame of a sex negative culture, a person fights back. This fight often leads to a rejection and denial of all traditional value systems. Eventually this "rebel" arrives at a place of experience which seems to be freed from society's restraint. Here in freedom we can do what we want, do as we please.

The period of freedom is often characterized by intense and frequent sexual encounters and a lifestyle focused upon parties, bars, and pleasure seeking. This unrestrained lifestyle offers an escape from the stress exerted by social and family expectations. A trap may develop here when intense sexual encounters become the only release from stress and tension. This can lead to health problems and may damage the ability to develop non-sexual intimacy with others.

The freedom stage is characterized by an emphasis upon individualism, autonomy, and materialism. This stage often extends for a number of years, sometimes producing self-centered patterns of behavior that are extremely difficult to overcome. It is also a period that includes the risk of developing serious drug and alcohol dependencies.

I am clearly suggesting that the freedom stage is not permanent and must be succeeded by another. My rationale rises from my experience and needs as well as from observing other people's lives. The unrestrained lifestyle of freedom remains a product of rebellion. I believe that this experience, when prolonged, produces loneliness and further damages our already weak system of relationship skills. To focus on pleasure and self, upon material gain and measurable achievement, further segregates our physical/ sexual selves from our spiritual/emotional selves. In the long run this is destructive. If we destroy ourselves by our freedom and rebellion we will have served to confirm society's negative attitudes toward gay people in particular and sexuality in general. The stages of freedom must not reinforce sex negative social attitudes. Therefore it is essential that we move on to the final stage.

Balance

Balance is needed for healthy self development that shall then become the foundation for a new sexual ethic. The balanced gay or lesbian person is the prophet of tomorrow. It is our balanced states of desire, emotional/physical, sexual/spiritual selves, that will then affect a real change in the social fabric of our culture. The homosexual example of balance brings liberty to a heterosexual system which has left men and women caught in the bondage of an archaic and inoperative ethic. The sex negative nature of our environment has left gay and non-gay people "out of balance."

Balance is a system of weight and counterweight, a state of equilibrium. Another dictionary definition of balance is the power to decide human fate and value. The achievement of equilibrium within the person brings harmony to the many factions of the self. Clearly the balanced person no longer experiences the split between the sexual and spiritual self. To be balanced in one area of life requires that all other areas achieve balance as well. The goal is internal harmony in which a sex positive attitude can develop and mature.

The lack of balance in the individual person has been amplified by the lack of relationship skills, the sex negative socio-religious environment, and the denial of self that has been the normative experience of many people growing up in America. This experience is considerably worse for gay and lesbian people.

The state of balance is possible only because of the experience of freedom. One may hope to move from guilt and fear directly to balance. Such a move would be a miraculous achievement. My best sense and experience confirms that balance comes only after the stage of rebellion and freedom. Furthermore, I am not at all sure that balance can be achieved without the rebellion, acting out and the experiences of sexual experimentation. Traditional values would reject this suggestion. This rejection is itself rooted in the fear of sexual expression. I believe that the pattern of development does move through the freedom stage and that it always does, whether we acknowledge it or not.

The sexual rebellion of every person is often a quiet and closeted affair. Yet it is there, violating all of the socio-religious codes of culture. Naming this process and giving it validity is essential if we are to achieve a sex positive society. Leading people out of guilt over who they are is the first step toward balance.

It is my perception that society fears we will all remain in the freedom stage of our growth to balance and further that this freedom will bring chaos to our social structures. The truth is that our social structures are already in chaos and must be allowed renewal. The truth is also that persons will seek balance beyond unrestrained freedom because they seek health and equilibrium.

The lack of balance in our lives and the need for balance can be clearly seen in countless situations of anonymous sexual encounters. One of the traits of freedom is unrestrained sexual activity, as we have already mentioned. Another phenomenon I observe is the tendency to keep sex partners separate from friends. Time and again I have heard gay men say "you can't sleep with your sister," meaning that sex is not to be shared with friends. What are we saying about ourselves and about sex? Why it is all right to share sex with strangers but not friends and acquaintances? Keeping sex anonymous and impersonal is a product of guilt and sex negative thinking. Further it points out the need for a balance between the impersonal relationship and the intimate one. I believe that it is healthy and natural for sex to be shared in the context of intimacy and friendship.

Someone once said to me, "If we have a sexual relationship I can no longer be a part of your church." This attitude of keeping sex separate from the rest of life and especially from religion, as in this case, demonstrates the out-of-balance state of our concepts regarding sexuality, relationship and spirituality.

The homosexual experience has been one of being out of balance on many levels. The attempt to live life on separate levels almost always ends in disaster. Great quantities of energy are required to segregate the many levels of our lives.

I will always remember the Episcopal priest from Virginia who told me how difficult it was to keep his gay friends and lover apart from his parish. It took a lot of energy to play the "straight" games while also attempting to maintain a separate and private life.

The fact that this man's public life was designed to negate the private one was producing a continuous state of tension and conflict.

Often the lack of balance and equilibrium between the various parts of one's life produces such tension that the person begins acting out self-destructive behavior in order to get caught. Getting caught allows the pretense and tension to end. This is often done in a passive/aggressive way so as to make someone else responsible. A case in point was my friend who pastored a small United Methodist church in central Michigan. He was gay and very closeted. He persisted in having sexual relations with boys in his church. He knew he was playing with fire. We even talked about it. When he was discovered and driven out of the church I could not help but feel as if that was what he wanted to happen. The result was increased guilt on his part and an overwhelming reinforcement of the sex negative attitude of the church in question. The people who were a part of this story only end up being greatly hindered in the ability to deal with homosexuality in the future.

We have lived for so long out of balance, that we assume an out-of-balance condition to be a normal one. Seeking balance in all areas of our lives may be an ambitious goal for anyone, yet I believe it to be both attainable and desirable.

If a sex positive ethic can be defined, it then can provide the possibility of achieving balance between sexuality and spirituality. Until these dimensions of life are brought to balance there is little hope for the rest of life coming to balance. This thesis is a powerful and controversial one as it insists upon the compatibility and mutual dependency of these two spheres, so let us tackle the task with fervor.

3
Sex Positive

Sex positive is an attitude and condition of living. It requires a sexual ethic that rests upon a positive Biblical base and takes its wisdom from the gifts of gay and lesbian people.

Our first task is to examine the essential components of a sexual ethic, without being legalistic. Previous attempts to define an ethic have ended by pronouncing right and wrong. Our goal is not to state right and wrong, but to shape boundaries that define sexual ethics.

Our second task is to extract a positive ethic for homosexuality from the Bible. This sounds like a monumental task. It is, however, a simple task which must be accomplished. Few people have attempted this: it is only further confirmation that a drastic split exists between the spiritual and sexual. It is with personal joy and confidence that I undertake this effort.

The third task is to examine relationship skills and contracts as essential ingredients in a sexual ethic that can work. Skills and contracts are practical tools that enable our concepts to take on flesh and function.

Our final task is to look at gay and lesbian prophets. I will state the case for our prophetic role and for new family structures. This will enable us to critique the heterosexual model of sex and family. It will provide an alternative to the current obsolete model.

Task One: Shaping the Ethics of Sexuality

The ethics of sexuality are an arena within life. They are a region bounded by specific principals; a country in which one can roam, explore, and grow to maturity. Freedom and permission to roam and explore are essential for healthy growth. Historically, our attempts to define a sexual ethic have been attempts to limit the exploration of sex. Rules which forbid change, experimentation and discovery do not produce a responsible sexual ethic. This ethic seeks to encourage diverse behavior rather than restrict behavior.

We all have grown up in a sex negative environment. We have not been given a sexual ethic. We have been given an ethical system of dos and don'ts with an overriding concern for procreation. We have received a code of morality which seeks to restrict behavior. The emphasis has been placed upon those things a person should not do rather than the things one should do. A "should not" ethic is fundamentally negative. It cannot produce a positive human response.

The following guidelines are boundaries within which we may find our own sexual behavior. My principal goals are to define our own behavior and to make healthy and responsible choices.

A sexual ethic must permit sexual diversity. Any ethic which does not permit diversity cannot meet the needs of a diverse human community. People are a mixture of more than one identity. People are not just heterosexual or homosexual. They are both, to varying degrees. A sexual ethic must allow for exclusive heterosexuality, exclusive homosexuality, bisexuality, asexuality, and transsexuality. We must acknowledge that this diversity exists everywhere. It is natural. This is a major first step. We cannot proceed without it.

The second step is to acknowledge variant sexual behavior as well as sexual identity. Not all people of similar sexual orientation act out their sexuality in the same way. A man and a woman in a traditional heterosexual relationship may choose to have sex solely in a "missionary position" and only between themselves. Another traditional male/female couple may indulge their fantasies to include any number of games, roles, or others. These two couples may share very similar social lives and may even share the same religious background. Yet, their sexual expression is very dissimilar.

Some gay men engage in very traditional sex roles while others express themselves in a variety of relationships. The same is true of lesbians.

Sexual behavior is a changing phenomenon. A person's sexual behavior goes through developmental stages. People at forty often find their sexual needs and appetites to be vastly different from those who are twenty. Couples also go through stages of alternately open and closed relationships.

A third guideline: a sexual ethic must seek to preserve and honor mutuality and consent. Freedom of choice, without coercion, may not be violated. Informed consent requires an intelligent and free choice. Sex between adults and children violates this concern for informed consent. Sexual acts which result from force or coercion do not have positive value.

I remember when I was coming out. I met a man I liked a lot. He invited me to dinner and plied me with alcohol. My drink would only be half gone: he would insist on "refreshing it." It didn't take long before I had to spend the night. Time and again this tactic has been used to weaken any possible defense or resistance. Often this coercive behavior is combined with guilt, creating a situation in which one or both parties seek to avoid responsibility for the sex act. Somehow getting drunk seemed to excuse any or all behavior while also allowing a person to avoid dealing with the sexual issues.

We have grown up in a culture that often seeks to avoid serious issues, especially sexual issues. We have learned to be indirect about sex. The gay bar scene is very sexual, yet, for the most part, people only suggest and imply what they want. "Do you want to stop by for a drink," can be translated, "I want you to come home with me," which means, "I want to have sex with you." The classic heterosexual line has been "Do you want to come up and see my etchings?" We are not taught or encouraged to be direct and honest. Try a direct approach sometime and notice shock. We have refined the practice of seduction when we should have refined communication. Clear and honest communication is the ally of mutual consent. This means that when the answer is no, it is no. It is inappropriate to ask "why?" Coercion and elaborate manipulative behavior often follow no. And, too often, no means "maybe."

Mutual consent goes beyond two persons sharing sexually. Once this choice is made, mutual consent must play a role in many other choices. Given the diversity of sexual experience and desire, one cannot assume that all partners want the same thing.

A feeling of rejection follows when a person declines an invitation to engage in a particular sexual act. A valid question about the moral character of a relationship can be asked when one partner insists upon a specific form of sex play, that excludes the desires of the other. This common situation leads us to the fourth point in the development of our sexual ethic.

A sexual ethic must enable growth toward maturity, as well as freedom to change. More simply stated, if I don't want to do what someone else wants, I must be allowed that choice. My fear or guilt must be acknowledged — if I cannot handle my partner's request, I need sensitivity, not judgment. Reinforcing guilt only reinforces a negative situation. Our sexual ethic must acknowledge that each person goes through many different stages of development. No two persons are likely to be in the same stage of experiential development at the same time.

When I reflect upon my own sexual maturation, I

clearly see how I have changed. What I am willing to do now is drastically different from what I was willing to do several years ago. What I may do ten years from now may be something I would never consider today. Our experience molds us. We are different because of our experience. Experience is cumulative. This sounds obvious; it must still be said.

Past efforts to formulate a sexual ethic have often assumed that a person is a certain way and is always that way. The sexual ethic we grew up with assumed heterosexuality. Some gay people even believed it and acted heterosexual. To all the world they appeared heterosexual. In time, they grew and changed, practicing sexual behavior they themselves condemned.

Our sexual ethic must recognize change and diversity. It must allow for a stage of rebellion and freedom, if there will ever be balance. Watching a person act out sexual behavior that appears negative and self-destructive is difficult. Sometimes one can point out this behavior; it usually has no effect upon the person. People must discover for themselves the values implicit in their behavior.

Our ethic must be flexible to accommodate diversity within each of us as well as between us. A rigid rule which seeks to apply to all people or to a person all the time does not work. A quick reflection upon our history and experience reveals this truth.

Positive sexual value is a fifth prerequisite for any sexual ethic. While this may appear obvious, it isn't to many. Most attempts to form sexual ethics have been built upon negative attitudes. Sex and sexual expression are positive and joyful components of human experience. Our fundamental attitude toward sex must be infused with positive values.

The future can be a time when sexual orientation and expression are considered precious components of life. We must be grateful for our sexuality. We can no longer seek to hide, restrict, or confine sex. We cannot continue to raise children who are embarrassed by their bodies.

A sexual ethic must give positive value to individuals. People should feel good about themselves and their bodies. I well recall my traumatic high school years. I hated gym class. I dreaded taking showers with the other boys. I was embarrassed to be seen by them. I grew up in a home where nudity is not expressed: it was very difficult to accept being naked around so many strangers.

Many of my early sexual encounters began by turning out the light. This practice was a product of guilt and shame about sex and our bodies.

I recall going to bed with a man who I thought handsome, mysterious, and very desirable. The experience with him was wonderful, yet he never undressed. At first I thought he was role-playing. I soon realized he was uncomfortable with his body. I thought he was wonderful; he did not. It was a long time before I could comfortably engage in sex with the lights on.

Our sex negative environment has devalued the person and denied the physical in our bodies. This does not lead to a healthy self-esteem.

Sexuality that values the person results in greater attention to individual needs and desires. Most sexual activity is focused upon the act, not the person. For instance, gay male sex strongly focuses on what one does or does not do, not who one is with. Individuals become experts in certain sexual activities and pride themselves on their performance. The other person is left out. When two experts engage with each other the goal appears to be refinement and self-pleasure rather than intimacy. The prevalent gay male focus upon technique and size results in impersonal sex. This only devalues the person.

Granting persons value requires another ingredient; a religious value system drawn from history and tradition. This value system should give positive value to the person. This system will be developed in the following section.

These guidelines for developing a sexual ethic allow us to make the following declarations:

1. Sex and sexual expression are positive parts of life.

2. Sexuality is a gift to be cherished, nurtured, expressed, and explored.

3. An important part of being a person is sexuality.

4. Sexual desires and behavior will change over time.

5. It is normal to go through many different stages of sexual development.

6. An individual's sexual expression will change over a lifetime.

7. People vary greatly in the nature, expression, and intensity of their sexuality.

This list could go on and on. We must learn to think positively about sex and sexuality, about our desires and our needs. For generations we have been taught to respond to our most personal and intimate selves with guilt, shame, and denial. This behavior must change if we are to live together in diversity.

A major reformation of western religion in general, and western Christianity in particular, is required. The church has misrepresented Biblical truth. It has created the foundation of our sex negative attitudes. It has attempted to contain, restrict, and deny sexual expression. No positive sexual ethic is possible until a Biblically based, sex positive foundation is built.

Our goal is to produce a positive Biblical foundation for gay and lesbian sexuality. We continue to live in an environment which uses religion and Scripture to deny homosexuality its legitimate and normal place in the human community. This assault has led gay and lesbian people to abandon religious tradition and, often, faith. This response should not be tolerated. Gay people must take back their birthright, their faith, their God, and their churches.

Reclamation of faith and history for gay people is our task. The message is addressed both to the Christian church, which has helped create sex negative attitudes, and gay Christians, who must fight back and speak the truth.

Our task is specific:

1. To state the Biblical truth about sex.
2. To include gay people in the Biblical truth.
3. To reverse tradition and free it from ignorance.
4. To allow a reunion of homosexuality and Christian spirituality.

"Can a person be a homosexual and a Christian?" The answer is absolutely yes.

I reject the notion of a "practicing" homosexual. Using the word "practicing" to qualify the word "homosexual" is a denial of physical sex. Gay people must reject the suggestion or requirement that they can be gay, but not engage in sex. This requirement, enforced by churches, is not acceptable.

"Practicing homosexual" is a sex negative term. It should always be challenged by sex positive people.

While I was speaking to two dozen clergy from various denominations, the following occurred:

After an hour of honest and intense sharing, a Presbyterian minister strongly protested that I was grossly unfair to the Presbyterian Church. I was condemning the church for their rejection of gay people. The minister said the church studied the issue in depth and had gone to great length to understand homosexuality and educate their people. I acknowledged that the Presbyterian Church had done significant work in this area, but gay men and lesbians were still denied ordination. My colleague protested strongly that this was not true and that gay people could be ordained in his denomination.

My response was a simple question, "Ordination is granted on what condition?" He replied, "Provided that the homosexual person remains celibate." The next question was obvious: "Are you willing to accept those same terms for yourself?" His response was also obvious, "Of course not, I am a normal heterosexual person."

The man's ignorance and blindness to the oppression of his argument made my point eloquently. I was outraged at him and argued that his position, if maintained by his denomination, would eventually destroy his church's credibility. To separate the physical person from the spiritual person is not acceptable.

Let us return to the primary question – How can a person be both Christian and homosexual?

The answer lies not only in the Bible but in the facts of human experience. There are millions of Christian homosexuals. Often, our existence is perceived as dependent upon the permission of denominational leaders. On the contrary, our existence and increasing visibility easily disproves that perception.

The endless and mindless debate about whether a person can be Christian and homosexual should cease. Our experience provides more than enough support for us to say resoundingly, "Yes, gay and lesbian Christians do exist." Let us proceed toward the goal of saying that this is a blessed and gracious gift from our Creator God.

We must begin by drawing some simple Biblical truths, conclusions drawn from the research listed in the index and supported by a lengthy list of sources. These essential conclusions should be common knowledge for Christians. Modern-day parents should teach these truths to their children.

1. Nowhere does the Bible discuss or evidence knowledge of homosexuality as a sexual orientation or lifestyle.

2. The Bible only mentions homosexual acts and always in the following contexts:

A. As part of the worship practices of other non-Jewish or non-Christian religions, i.e. Canaanite religion and Greek mystery cults.

B. As abusive and violent behavior such as rape.

3. The condemnation of these acts is a rejection of all things pertaining to these other religions and not a rejection of the sexuality implicit in these acts. The issue was never sexuality but rather idolatry. (Conservative Christians in America are fond of calling homosexuality an abomination. The word abomination literally means idolatry.)

4. Many problems exist in the translation of certain New Testament words which leave the meaning obscure. The obscurity has become an open door through which people have introduced the sex negative cultural baggage. This has become a cultural gloss overlaying the Biblical text.

5. Most profoundly, Jesus never said a word regarding homosexuality.

With these five points we move toward a sex positive Biblical base.

The task begins with a rejection of past Biblical ignorance. The blessing is that the argument for gay Christians has a more credible Biblical basis than has the argument against gay Christians. The conservative tide against the gay Christian movement and gay people in general will fail. It will collapse under the weight of unsound Biblical principles. The agent of this collapse will be truth.

1. The Bible is a storehouse of rich examples of sexual/sensual union between spirit and flesh.

2. The Bible is the source for models of same sex loving.

3. The Bible is the source for liberating the human spirit from old legalisms.

4. The Bible offers a specific example of a sexual minority person's unique and special union with God.

5. The Bible is a guide that helps our sex positive ethics unit with history and tradition.

The Sensuality of Scripture

The sex negative tradition we received has screened out the very physical and sensual nature of Scripture. A rediscovery of Biblical truth reveals that the people of the Bible were very sexual folk. The Old Testament narrative is filled with passion. Men of old had many wives. Their stories reveal nothing akin to our Western nuclear family. A lusty vitality fills Scripture with tales of passion, sex, love, and violence. It is important for us to see the humanity of these people. Too often we seek to separate the physical and spiritual in stories from Scripture. Only when the two are in union do we see the majesty of the message. How can we identify with the message unless we can see our experience reflected by it?

It would serve us all well if we read aloud the Song of Songs (Song of Solomon). We should hear of the love between lovers, from our pulpits. Here the sensual self is spoken of in a prayerful language.

> Upon my bed by night I sought him whom my soul loves; I sought for him, but found him not; I called him, but he gave no answer. 'I will rise now and go about the city, in the streets and in the squares; I will seek him whom my soul loves.' I sought him, but found him not. The watchmen found me, as they went about in the city. 'Have you seen him whom my soul loves?' Scarcely had I passed them, when I found him whom my soul loves. I held him, and would not let him go until I had brought him into my mother's house, and into the chamber of her that conceived me. (Song of Solomon 3:1-4, RSV)

This could have been written by any modern gay man; his longing for love, his nights of cruising the streets, and his search for the beloved. The quest includes a longing to take the lover home to mother. We look to the New Testament and find the Kingdom of God referred to as a wedding feast, a sumptuous banquet.

Few things are more sensual than a bountiful feast.

The Kingdom is also discussed as a marriage between a bride and her husband. The point is the sexual/sensual nature of the message, not the heterosexual nature of the image. For those who wish to raise the heterosexual model here, I say wait. A Biblical model for same sex bonding will be offered.

Jesus' ministry is filled with touch and feeling. How I long for modern Christians to be free to touch, weep, embrace, kiss, and hold as did the founder of our faith. The Gospel writers speak of the disciple whom Jesus loved; he pictured Jesus laying upon his breast. We are making no case for Jesus being homosexual. Jesus was physical, sensual, and did not fear his human nature.

The cardinal doctrine of the Christian faith rests in the union of spirit and flesh. "The word became flesh and dwelt among us, full of grace and truth," (John 1:14, RSV). How can a religion which was born in this union have wandered so far from its base truth?

If it is true and the spirit has taken on flesh, it must also be true that this is an inclusive statement. The spirit is immersed in flesh, regardless of race, gender, or sexual orientation. It also means that the spirit did not stop at the neck or the waist. It embraces all the flesh.

The witness of Scripture is itself sex positive. Teaching this to our children would prevent the guilt many of us have about the physical and sexual. It would eliminate much mental stress and illness, the product of the present attitude.

Our use of Scripture must offer balance. We must

avoid selective and partisan interpretations in favor of balanced and holistic ones.

The following Biblical examples provide balance to an out-of-balance tradition.

I am not going to say that they were lovers. The two most powerful images of bonding, love, and devotion within Scripture are same sex-images – Ruth and Naomi, and Jonathan and David.

Same-Sex Pair Bonding

Ruth and Naomi. It is curious that for generations the heterosexual marriage rite has quoted from the story of Ruth. "Entreat me not to leave you or to return from following you; for where you go I will go, and where you lodge I will lodge; your people shall be my people and your God my God; where you die I will die, and there I will be buried," (Ruth 1:16-17, RSV).

These words have been spoken millions of times between a man and woman, while ignoring their context. It seems clear that the depth and beauty of this bonding must lead to transcendence of the narrow limitations within heterosexual models. Further, this same-sex model can give new meaning to male/female unions.

Jonathan and David. I am tired of arguments about whether David and Jonathan were homosexuals. There is no argument. The Scripture clearly indicates a deep, powerful, and physical love between them. Few places in literature, either sacred or secular, offer a more profound model of union. All one has to do is read the story.

"The soul of Jonathan was knit to the soul of David. . ." (I Samuel 18:1, RSV). This seems far more bonded than most homosexual love relationships. ". . . and Jonathan loved him as his own soul," (18:1).

The Bible says that "Jonathan made a covenant with David, because he loved him," (18:3). Jonathan stripped himself and gave David his clothes and his armor and his sword, in full view of all the people. The love between Jonathan and David is expressed in an oath and covenant as well as a physical union. "David rose . . . and fell on his face to the ground, bowed three times and they kissed one another, and wept with one another," (20:41).

Few words in all the world's literature can compare with this epithet: "Jonathan lies slain upon the high places. I am distressed for you my brother Jonathan; very pleasant have you been to me; your love to me was wonderful, passing the love of women," (II Samuel 1:26, RSV).

At the beginning of his lament, David says this lament should be taught to the people. If only we had taught young men about the love of Jonathan and David, perhaps we would have grown up as free as they to kiss and hold and weep. If modern concepts of masculinity could recapture this sex positive message, much healing would take place.

Let us take two more steps towards freedom and towards a balanced view of the Bible and sexuality. This balanced view requires an understanding of the sensuality of Scripture. A Biblical rationale must leave behind the legalisms of the past.

And it must speak a message to all sexual minorities – i.e. gay, lesbian, transsexual, asexual, bisexual – which affirms our place in God's kingdom.

Breaking Free of the Law

I rarely understand the message of evangelical, conservative, and fundamental preachers. They plea with passion for people to abide by the laws of the Old Testament holiness code. This plea makes no sense for Christians who claim that Christ has freed them from Old Testament law.

Efforts to return to the sexual proscriptions of the Old Testament are motivated by greed for political and economic gain, not by faith or moral concern. Preachers have long used a message of fear and condemnation to produce guilt. Guilty "sheep" follow better and give more money. As harsh as this sounds, I believe it to be true. When this power motive is attached to ignorance, a dangerous combination is created.

To a modern gay Christian, the extent of Biblical ignorance and illiteracy within the Christian churches is deeply disturbing. The New Testament message is that we are free from the law. This freedom is found in Jesus, who has broken the bondage of that law. To understand this freedom, let us look at a passage from Hebrews.

"When there is a change in the priesthood, there is necessarily a change in the law as well," (Hebrews 7:12, RSV).

Christ is presented as the new high priest. In Christ, the law is fulfilled and in Christ, a new law is established. This is the law of love.

To love means to allow to be, to accept a person as they are. To love is to grant the freedom to be. A person can grow and change only with freedom. The entire New Testament is a discussion of the meaning of love revealed in the context of the life and teachings of Jesus. His life expresses and defines love. Why would any representative of the Christian faith seek to enforce the Hebrew law? If Christ has brought a change in the law, then the old law has no power over us.

It is folly for television preachers to claim to be born anew while clinging so desperately to a law they themselves cannot abide. It is clear that the motive of the religious right wing is not religious or moral concern, but economic and political power. The tragedy is that they gain both. Why? Because they preach fear. They use the fear of sexuality to condemn gay people and others.

We must reject their moral code. It does not fit human realities. It does not conform to Biblical truth. It is not loving. It has failed to bring healing to the lives and relationships of gay and non-gay people alike.

The kingdom of fear, reinforced by the religious right, is in a process of collapse. There has been a change in the priesthood and in the law. The gay Christian message is more closely aligned with the intent of the Scripture and of Christ himself. Our message of truth will topple their kingdom of lies.

As gay Christians, let us take the next significant step. Let us present a Biblical message that addresses the gay experience in a powerful and positive way.

Here is the Biblical foundation for a homosexual's place in the Kingdom of God. It is a positive word in the midst of a sex negative tradition.

> Let not the foreigner who has joined himself to the Lord say, "The Lord will surely separate me from his people"; and let not the eunuch say, "Behold I am a dry tree." For thus says the Lord: "To the eunuchs who keep my sabbaths, who choose the things that please me and hold fast my covenant, I will give in my house and within my walls a monument and a name better than sons and daughters; I will give them an everlasting name which shall not be cut off.
>
> "And the foreigners who join themselves to the Lord, to minister to him, to love the name of the Lord, and to be his servants, every one who keeps the sabbath, and does not profane it, and holds fast my covenant – these I will bring to my holy mountain, and make them joyful in my house of prayer; their burnt offerings and their sacrifices will be accepted on my altar; for my house shall be called a house of prayer for all peoples. Thus says the Lord God, who gathers the outcasts of Israel, I will gather yet others to him besides those already gathered." (Isaiah 56:3-8 RSV)

This text speaks to two groups of people, the foreigner and the eunuch. The foreigner represents all outsiders and all outcasts. The eunuch represents a minority defined by their sexual difference from the rest of Israel: eunuchs were outcasts due to their physical condition.

The message is clear. Both the outsider and the eunuch will receive "a monument and a name better than the name of sons and daughters . . . an everlasting name which shall not be cut off." God's house will include all people. Gay and lesbian Christian movements around the world are a fulfillment of this text. We are modern eunuchs. We have been cut off from the household of faith. The message of restoration speaks to us.

It is time for gay Christians to debate the religious right-wing movement and "moral majority." It is time for us to claim our place and heritage. We affirm that those who are the most outcast will be the most exulted.

A counterpart to this message is found in Matthew's Gospel:

> But he said to them, "Not all men can receive this saying, but only those to whom it is given. For there are eunuchs who have been so from birth, and there are eunuchs who have been made eunuchs by men, and there are eunuchs who have made themselves eunuchs for the sake of the kingdom of heaven. He who is able to receive this, let him receive it." (Matthew 19:11-12 RSV)

Jesus is teaching about marriage. To the question, "should all marry?" Jesus gives a very strange answer. He says, "Not all men can receive this saying, but only to those to whom it is given. For there are eunuchs who have been so from birth. . ." Jesus concludes:

"He who is able to receive this, let him receive it." This saying only occurs here in Matthew's account of this teaching. Mark's account omits this reference to eunuchs. I have found no interpretation of these verses.

I believe that Jesus was speaking to those who, from birth, have been sexually different. Sexual minorities can receive this message. This is an acknowledgment of sexual minorities; an acknowledgment that not all people can receive the meaning of this saying.

This interpretation has been hidden for generations. It is now a time of prophetic fulfillment; a time for gay people to claim their heritage and their faith. The Isaiah and Matthew passages are important parts of our presentation of truth to the church. We have moved, systematically, from a negative and uninformed view of the Bible to one which supports and nurtures sexual diversity. This process has maintained the integrity of the Scripture.

Historically, gay people have rejected the Bible, together with the church which has rejected us. We can now reclaim our faith, and interpret it through the wisdom of our experience. This process challenges the existing structure of the church. It strikes at the foundations of concepts which have been built upon ignorance and falsehood.

It is time for us to preach a gospel which brings good news to gay people. We are returning to the faith and to the promise that "we shall have names better than the names of sons and daughters."

Building Gay Relationships and Community

A healthy gay person is an essential component in a healthy gay community. Healthy people have left behind the guilt, fear, and shame of a sex negative tradition. We have moved through the process of rebellion and freedom to balance. Balance for us is a life which is positive and has a sex positive Biblical tradition. The steps we have just proposed must be taken for health and wholeness to be achieved. There can be no successful gay rights movement without the sexual and the spiritual integration. This union produces the energies and commitment essential to the human rights struggle.

When we leave behind the sex negative tradition we leave behind many of the rules and regulations that society has used to constrain relationships. Social instruments developed in an atmosphere of guilt and fear will not survive in a climate of freedom and questioning. Gay relationships must forge new structures if they are to succeed and offer hope to non-gay relationships. Non-gay relationships also need redemption from sex negative traditions.

A sex positive climate enables relationships to develop free from the sex games so common in a guilt-ridden environment. Sex positive relationships will include the characteristics of our sexual ethic. The fact that our spirituality can accommodate the diversity of sexual experience reflects a new age. Openness, honesty, and trust are the values of a sex positive person.

The most significant product of a sex positive approach is the abandonment of traditional sexual roles. The traditional roles learned by men and women have served to enforce negative attitudes about sex. They have damaged our self-esteem. Our positive approach to relationships values mutuality and interdependence.

Thesis: Sex positive relationships draw energy from the union of sex and spirit. This energy creates the possibility for healthy people and a healthy community.

We no longer need the social scripts given to us in childhood. We have removed the "Dos" and "Don'ts" of sex and relationship. In their place, we have a system which encourages individual choice and evaluation. We are free from oppressive rules applied to all. In their place is a value system bound only by the guidelines of our sexual ethic.

Time and time again, people have asked me, as a pastor, what is right and what is wrong. My response has always been to point them toward honesty. I ask them what they want and why they want it. Over and over again couples want me to tell them that an exclusive sexual relationship is what they need to build a stable, loving union. Two people can have an exclusive relationship, if that is what both individuals want. My warning is always: "Be sure that is what you want." If two people seek a sexually exclusive relationship because it is a "necessity" or because it is more moral, then they will not be successful. What usually results is a dishonest union in which two people pretend exclusivity, while each sneaks around having outside affairs. The climate of dishonesty erodes the love and trust between two people.

I counsel couples to define an agreement for their relationship. It should be based upon their individual needs and wants. The agreement will change over time as each person changes and as the relationship develops.

Many researchers, like Andrew Mattison and David McWhirter in their study *The Male Couple,* have defined the stages of relationship development. My own observation and experiences parallel their findings. Sexual behavior changes as the relationship changes. A couple will often begin their relationship closed. After a period of time, it may become open to sexual sharing with others. This open period may be followed by another closed period. My professional experience confirms this to be especially true for male couples, and increasingly true for female couples.

The moment the discussion turns to sexual openness one can expect another sex negative Biblical argument. That argument is Biblical teaching about adultery and marriage. With our sex positive approach to the Bible in mind, let us add another important ingredient to our sexual ethic.

Biblical discussion regarding adultery proscribes the sexual behavior of women and says very little about men. It is always the woman who is caught in adultery, not the man. Again, the heterosexual model is not relevant to the homosexual relationship.

The Biblical approach to adultery is sexist and misogynist. It needs to be reformed. The experience of homosexuals will provide the reformation and a new, positive value system – one which adds balance to an out-of-balance tradition.

The old rules for relationships do not meet gay and lesbian needs. Fitting people into rigid forms is the antithesis of our ethic. The old rules do not encourage contracts and agreements that are specific and unique to each couple. The old rules seek to fit all couples into one agreement. Each couple should define the agreement which works for them. Many will condemn this approach, but it is inherently more honest and more loving.

This is not an "anything goes" approach to sexual ethics. It is a responsible ethic derived from positive guidelines and Biblical tradition.

Gay men and lesbians do live by this ethic and demonstrate healthy lifestyles. All I have said would be meaningless if it were only academic or abstract. People are living this lifestyle today. These guidelines are derived from human experience. They are a product of the struggle for human rights and dignity.

Gay and lesbian people have been forced to break the rules to be true to our own nature. We have arrived at a point in our history when we can write a Christian ethic which fits our reality. Our ethic preserves the truth and meaning of our tradition. We have successfully added our history to a tradition which has excluded us. Radical reformation is the result: a reformation that is greatly needed and welcome.

Gay and Lesbian Prophets

Gay and lesbian people have a prophetic role. We

are prophets and we speak a bold truth.

We are:

1. Providing a critique of the heterosexual model from outside it;

2. Providing new models of family;

3. Providing freedom from sex determined roles;

4. Providing new structures for all relationships based upon a sex positive value system.

The history and experience of homosexuals is a vantage point from which to review traditional sexual ethics and relationships. Standing outside the traditional values and prescribed roles for men and women, homosexual people have seen the distortion and abuse suffered by those who seek to conform to values alien to their experience. So many of us have attempted to be what we are not. The years of denial have taken their toll in our health and self esteem.

The struggle and suffering have produced wisdom, insight, and strength. Through the suffering we have viewed the inadequacy of tradition. We speak now of a new way that enables all people to build lives and relationships of trust and honesty. Our message gives hope to women and men who have found themselves denying themselves in order to accommodate traditional expectations.

The clearest way we can critique traditional family structures is to combine our experience with another positive Biblical teaching, to create a new, yet ancient, family model.

Family Redefined

In Matthew 12:46-50, Jesus is interrupted by one of the disciples. The disciple tells him that his mother and brothers are outside and wish to speak to him. Jesus replies, "Who is my mother, and who are my brothers? Whoever does the Will of God is my brother, and sister, and mother." (RSV)

Here is a powerful truth which can deliver gay men and lesbians from the pain of family rejection. Jesus defined true family as those who do God's will. This family produces love, justice, and acceptance among all people. Our model for family is a fellowship, a commonwealth of people who nurture and support our lives. This family may include blood relatives, but it certainly extends far beyond the traditional family unit.

Gay people have formed new family units, composed of caring, supporting people. These units fulfill the need to affirm, celebrate, and symbolize our lifestyle. New family units gather on holidays and anniversaries to offer the love often withheld by our blood relatives. The success and longevity of these units offer hope to all people who have been cut off from their traditional families. Individuals have been cut off from families because they are homosexual, have engaged in premarital sex, have conceived children as single parents, have united with persons of other races or creeds. This rejection is rooted in fear and reinforced by sex negative traditions.

The new family model provides a symbol of hope for all rejected by traditional families. Our family model gains authority from a positive Biblical foundation.

We have seen how gay men and lesbians have challenged the values and structure of our society. Our witness confronts western religious teaching. We bring our truth to shed new light on Scripture and tradition. Our existence gives us a prophetic role, calling into question our exclusion from the church, state, and family. Gay and lesbian people of faith pronounce judgment upon every church which excludes them. The growing gay Christian movement offers reformation and redemption from old fears, Biblical ignorance, and the bondage of a sex negative tradition.

We are prophets by our presence and our word. Our labor and influence have brought new scholarship to the ancient Biblical debates. This scholarship has discovered a clear truth and brought new integrity to Biblical teaching.

Our message is being spoken in every quarter of the Christian church. The birth of the Universal Fellowship of Metropolitan Community Churches (UFMCC) in 1968 has occasioned this revolution. History will no doubt credit the Reverend Troy D. Perry, founder of the UFMCC, as one of the prophets who turned the Christian church from a sex negative to a sex positive tradition.

Talking and writing about the union of the sexual and spiritual is ultimately worthless unless it can be presented as flesh and blood. What follows is a case history of sexual spiritual merger.

This case history precedes all of my understanding of the merger of sex and spirit. It is also the foundation of my reflection upon scripture and tradition. This foundation is consistent with Christian theology and tradition. We reflect upon experience and, then, write our theology, doctrine, and Scripture. The Bible is a faith history, the recording of individuals' views of history and its meaning. I affirm that God was the inspiration and motivation for such writing. I also affirm that that same God is the inspiration and motivation for this writing. Our lives and work represent modern Scripture, which in time may be given the same authority as the ancient record.

4
Sexual/Spiritual Merger: A Case History

The best stories are true stories. There is no better way to describe the meaning and importance of sexual/spiritual merger than to present a true story. What follows are experiences that span twenty-five years. At the age of thirteen or fourteen I began a private search to know God in the most personal and intimate of ways.

The beginning of this case history establishes both my symbol of God's presence and my method of affirming that presence. The story then presents a period some seven years later, when I was about 21 years old. The symbol of God's presence was vividly revealed to me at that age and became essential to my life.

The final stage is a merger of the personal and historical symbol of God's presence with its sexual expression. All the volatile energy of spirit and sex exploded within me, integrating my life and the life of another man. The merger of sexuality and spirituality defined my being and focused my sense of self. It allowed me to grasp the future. The merger of sexual and spiritual selves stands at the center of the process of movement to wholeness and self-integration. The merger moves us to the prospect of an important and exciting future – a future filled with life and transformation.

This story demonstrates a sex positive experience. It makes real all we have discussed.

The story is the most intimate I have ever shared. Its message is essential to my meaning. I share it with the knowledge that I become extremely vulnerable. I stand naked before a world which is not equipped to accept such honesty.

As a preacher's kid (PK), I was exposed to unusual situations. People treated me with the fake piety they prepared for Daddy. I grew up in church, you might say. I like to say that I was born on a pew. Worship three times a week was normal for our conservative, evangelical Christianity.

Besides being a pastor, Daddy was a television star. While I did not realize the impact it had at the time, my father was a pioneer religious broadcaster. The names of my father's friends did not impress me. Jerry Falwell was just another preacher. When my daddy talked him into taking over his television show in Lynchburg in 1958, I did not think it a significant event.

People like Billy Graham and Oral Roberts were family friends. Daddy knew them. I thought very little of their presence; it was normal for them to be there. I recall being in awe of my father's friends only twice. The first time was when Roy Rogers and Dale

Evans came to Washington in 1956 at my father's invitation. It was another revival, only this time my hero was coming. Little did I know then that my love for my cowboy hero was a part of my emerging sexual identity. The second time was when Daddy was invited to the White House by Dwight and Mamie Eisenhower. I was upset with my father for not taking me along to David Eisenhower's eighth birthday party. I wanted to go more to be with my cowboy hero than the President. Daddy had promised Roy and Dale a trip to the White House.

So I grew up before thousands of people. I grew up on radio and television. Christian faith was as deeply rooted in my being as were eating and sleeping.

The history of growing up gay in evangelical America makes good material for a book in itself. It is the story of a sex negative world, of the inability of Christian people to honestly face sexual diversity.

While I never questioned this faith or the reality of God, I did desire that God make himself especially real to me. I wanted a sign. I remember my quest for a special sign from God in great detail. I sat on the front steps of our home in Alexandria, Virginia. It was a clear summer evening. The brightness of the evening stars was just above the Virginia Hills development. I sat gazing into a moonless sky and began my conversation with God.

"God, it's me, Larry. You know that I believe in you. (pause) You know that I love you. (pause) You know how faithful I have tried to be. (pause)" Then I would make my innocent petition.

"God, it would be wonderful if you sent a shooting star right over my house." (pause) I would stare at the sky knowing that any second one would appeal "God, it is not as if I am asking for a miracle. wouldn't do that and you know that. I won't stop believing in you if you don't send a star, but really it's a simple request. It would mean so much to me." (pause) Something would move in the sky, and my heart would quicken: a red light blinking next to a green one, an airplane. So I would try again, this time strengthening my case a bit.

"God, you do know that a shooting star is not really a star, it is a meteorite and they are falling through the atmosphere constantly all over the world. There is no reason why one shouldn't just happen to enter the atmosphere right over Alexandria." I was very willing to make an ordinary occurrence an important faith event. God would surely appreciate that.

Plea after plea, rational argument upon rational argument, resulted in no star. I was not discouraged. I supposed that God was probably busy with important things. He couldn't arrange for my star right then. Nevertheless, I would spend many summer nights making the same request. I saw many meteorites, but never on demand.

I grew in years and sophistication. I stopped making my request. I continued to hold my strong faith in God. I continued to live a life which appeared deeply religious. I was not able to acknowledge that beneath this pious surface a war raged between my faith and the growing awareness of my sexuality.

The conflict consumed me, destroying much of my life. It altered forever the world I knew. The destruction and transformation of myself ushered in a whole new creation. I would live at the point of conflict and its resolution. I did not doubt that I loved men. The depth and power of that attraction has never diminished. Yet, it took many years to end the war of spirit and flesh. The fight was a solitary one.

The world was working hard with the church to keep my sexuality and my spirituality far apart. I did not know that God was working harder to reconcile the two. God would win. I did not have the star I so longed for. I don't even know why I longed for a star. Maybe because a star over Bethlehem set the standard for the revelation of God's presence. Maybe I was just arrogant and wanted as much as the wise men got. What seemed to me then as arrogance now is affirmed to me as healthy self esteem and a faith which expects action.

Still, no star.

Nineteen Sixty-five

My life couldn't have gotten much worse than it was in the summer of 1965. I was no kid. I was a junior at Michigan State University. The war in my flesh was at an all-time high. Life did not make much sense. My spirit was telling me that God wanted me to go into the ministry, the world was telling me that that was impossible. The reason was clear – I was a homosexual. There was no room for me. I couldn't understand God's persistence. Why was God asking for the impossible? The battle would rage for a few more years. I could only let it boil in me, while I tried to live my life. I still stared at the night skies of Michigan in midwinter, but dared not ask for anything. My spirit wanted an intimate and personal sign: a communion with God that would transport me out of conflict. I wanted to be told that I was God's own.

I went home for the summer. Life was much changed. Mother and Father were never together. Home was strange. A storm cloud dominated every day. My twin brother and I decided to go to Maine and visit our best friend and his family. We left the heat of Washington D.C. and headed for New England. The trip should have brought some peace of mind. The countryside was beautiful and I began to feel a sense of history. I was enchanted by the sight of the sea, the rugged coast of Maine, and the lobsters.

The escape didn't last long. In the midst of hay-cutting season I had a major asthma attack. I am sure that the hay was only one factor. The emotional stress at home was another. I could barely breathe. In a panic, my brother put me in the car and we drove home. The long trip to D.C. brought only a modest amount of relief. And it added weariness to my body.

I will never forget the moment I saw my mother's face. She was at work when we arrived. I was breathing somewhat better, but I knew that the world had changed. I asked what was wrong. When she replied nothing, I knew everything was wrong. We could not pretend with one another. In tears, she told me that Daddy had gone to Mexico and gotten a divorce. He married a woman we all knew. Then the other shoe fell, I had a half-brother who was twelve.

In that instant, I understood everything. In a flash I remembered a tragic day when my mother had packed her bags and left. Dad retrieved her. I had never known why. Now the years of her quiet pain all seemed clear.

The war between flesh and spirit was not mine alone. A preacher was not allowed to be a sexual being. There was no room, nor forgiveness for my father. Now I understood why the world of television, radio, and churches had all fallen away. Many of the mysteries of my adolescent years now made sense.

My world seemed to end that day along with my innocence. The sexual and spiritual were on a collision course toward union. I did not understand for some years how this union would be holy.

The next month was bitter. The emotional upheaval was intensified by asthma. I was gravely ill at home while mother attempted to live and manage her pain. I could not bear her sorrow nor her tears in the night. I was angry at Dad and angry at God. Life seemed close to ending, yet it went on.

I was on the threshold of a new beginning. My asthma got better. I was up and out of the house. Summer was drawing near its end.

What could the fall hold for me? How could I return to Michigan State? There was no money. Mother could not help me and I could no longer expect Dad to carry the burden. I did not want to see him. How could I still believe that God was in this? How could God allow this to happen? Questions raged within me, each one competing with the other. They prevented sleep, and deepened my despair.

One night, I walked through the parking lot behind the high-rise apartment we lived in. I walked into the wooded picnic area. I had often sought male companionship there in the darkness. Occasionally I had found someone, found a brief moment of sexual pleasure to divert my thoughts.

This time was different. I was not interested in finding a sex partner. I was wrestling with my life, my God, and my future.

Tears steamed down my face. I wept in despair. How could I continue my education? How could God still be calling me to the ministry?

I pleaded aloud: "Tell me it's okay. Tell me you will take care of me; tell me you are there." Through my wet eyes I pleaded with the heavens. Then it came. With a brightness as intense as any star I had ever seen. It traveled from horizon to horizon. It was "my star," my answer. How did I know it? I knew because my spirit leaped with joy. I laughed, and all the tension and struggling left my body. A sweet peace filled me. I returned to the apartment, and from that moment I approached life with a quiet confidence.

I believe that every human being has some intimate spiritual experience which occupies a central part in their life. This was mine. It immediately connected my childhood seeking with my present and my future. God was alive again. I could not know how this star would again heal my life, end my struggle, and merge my sexual and spiritual selves.

It was just a meteorite, but it was mine. My symbol of God's nearness and concern for me came when I most needed it. I had to be bailed out of my hopelessness. When you hit the bottom, the deepest part of life's experience, God is deeper still. The very sign I had wanted, I received. God met me on my terms yet I was never the one in control. The event was one of those focusing moments in which ordinary life occurrences are interpreted through faith. Events become symbols and interpret experiences yet to come. This focus is called a miracle.

Nineteen Eighty-two – Erotic Prayer

I am now a happy, well-adjusted homosexual and a minister within the Universal Fellowship of Metropolitan Community Churches. My life is open and I am "out" about my sexuality. I am active in the political and social gay community of Washington, D.C. One would think that I had it "all together." I am a "professional homosexual" teaching and counseling others, so that they may claim and appreciate the gift of their sexuality.

There were still deep places within me which needed healing. I had had an unsuccessful relationship that ended after seven years. But I did have a successful professional life and a new relationship. There was yet another event that would bring further focus to my life. One more miracle would occur achieving sexual/spiritual union.

It was the summer of 1982. I was not looking for anything other than some rest, a chance to escape from the rush of Washington and the pressures of the ministry. I headed for Rehoboth Beach, Delaware.

Rehoboth was the beach of my childhood. It was peaceful and quiet. It had grown up enough to have a gay bar, a good gay restaurant, and a gay beach. One night, I went to the bar alone. I only wanted to have a beer, relax, and enjoy the beautiful bodies as they danced. I had no intention of meeting anyone.

I was standing on the patio when my eyes caught the eyes of another. He was dark-haired, bearded, with deep, dark eyes. I noticed his denim and boots and was immediately interested. One can only take so much of the "preppie" look. In other words, he fit one of my fantasies.

We made no move toward one another for several minutes. Glance followed glance in deepening intensity. I moved to him and we began the usual conversation: "Hi, where are you from?" "DC, where else." And so on.

There was something about him, a deepness in his eyes, the kind that makes you nervous. He had a penetrating power which stripped me naked, and seduced the spirit along with the flesh.

He asked, "Are you a minister?" I always give honest answers to questions; I said yes. This usually begins long discussions about religion or the Bible: discussions I do not wish to have in bars. He did not ask more. He simply replied that he always had a way of meeting clergy. We talked for a while until we reached that awkward moment when both people know the issue of sex is at hand. "Do you have a place?" he asked. I replied yes. "Can we go there?"

I hesitated. Part of me did not want to sleep with anyone that night. I wanted company, yes, but a pensive spirit within wanted to think, ponder, and walk along the surf. Part of me wanted to explore this stranger who seemed to easily penetrate my spirit. I said yes. We drove to the beach house I was using. At first, everything was ordinary. We climbed to the loft where there were only twin beds. This was awkward for two large men, so we moved to the floor. After a few various oral/genital configurations in the narrow space between beds, I felt I was in a comedy and my sexual interest faded.

We stopped. He put his arms around me and said, "Let's go make love on the beach." This must be everyone's fantasy: at least those of us raised on Hollywood romance. We took a blanket and he led me to the beach.

Outside sex always carries with it the risk of being discovered. This does, however, add some thrill. We were far from town: around us were only sand dunes and sea. It was very late, so all the beach houses were dark.

There was no moon and the black sky was without a hint of clouds. There were a multitude of stars. Rarely had I seen the Milky Way so clearly. It was like a highway through the heavens, a swath of white sparkles across an ebony field.

We lay in the sand on our blanket. I soon forgot the sand and its grit, along with the possibility of discovery. In the freedom of this grand open space, I wanted this man. I wanted to be inside of him. He had been gently kissing all of me while I lay gazing at the stars. I rolled over and without a word his body moved beside me, then beneath. I slid onto him effortlessly and began the rhythmic ride to orgasm. I took my time. Then, with the breeze off the sea caressing my back and the surging surf in rhythm with my thrusts, I flowed into him.

In stillness, we lay together for an endless time. It was as if we fell asleep although in fact I don't think we did; it was a kind of reverie. He repeated the scene. He mounted me and drove deeply into my flesh. We gave no thought to lubricant or to the presence of sand. We only thought of the naturalness of each other and the deep intimacy of flesh and spirit. Between the several orgasms we talked. We talked about God and love and faith and our confident hope about life.

The time passed, and no one came down the beach. The stars only seemed to intensify their piercing points of light.

My partner asked me to lay back. He promised an exceptional experience. I almost refused; I had no more sexual energy left – I thought. We gave ourselves to each other when it seemed there was nothing left to give. The warmth of his mouth and its gentle persistent rhythm aroused me again. I laid there, on my back, staring into an incredible sky while this man proceeded to give my genitals his attention with passion and commitment.

Something beyond words began to happen. I felt the earth under me, solid, as I saw the heavens turning above me. We felt like one unit, the earth, the heavens, and I. My mind began to expand the scene and my erect organ seemed to raise not just into my partner's mouth, but from the earth into the heavens. A high monument, stirring the stars. Tears filled my eyes as I began to feel God's presence with me, with us. I dared to pray. "God, it's me. I want you to have all of me. I want my semen to flow as a gift to you.

My body fluid; intimate symbol of life, to pour out in gratitude. Receive all of me." It was as if my partner was God drawing life from me. I was loving both this man and God. Then I saw more keenly still the white flow of the Milky Way. My prayer went on. "Let my semen flow into the Milky Way. I want each sperm to add to the billions of stars." A pulse began to throb within me. The surging sea and my body rhythm were one. I began to seek to give myself to God. No longer could I differentiate between the sexual experience and my prayer life. In the spirit, I prayed. In a new language of ecstasy, I spoke. Some call it tongues, others the language of private prayer. I knew it to be a private communication between God and me.

Everything peaked, I filled my partner's mouth with semen. In the mystery of my faith and fantasy, I flowed into the Milky Way. At my orgasm a brilliant shooting star traveled the length of the Milky Way. My sexual gift had been received. God had touched me more intimately than ever before. The symbol of my childhood seeking had returned to heal the gap between sexuality and spirituality. The act was holy, my flesh was holy, and a holy loving God embraced all of me, without exclusion or exception. It was a silent, holy night.

I never saw the man on the beach again. I believed God had sent him to complete my journey. Now the little boy who used to beg for stars was an adult gay male who knew that his homosexuality was a gracious and powerful gift from God. This gift must be shared, to continue healing the lives of gay men and women everywhere.

The merger taught me a truth which must be shared. At the core of each of us lies our spiritual and sexual selves. These two must become one. The union of sexuality and spirituality is essential for all people. We shall never understand or use our spiritual gifts until we come to terms with our sexual selves. We shall never know the depth, power, or purpose of our sexuality until we merge it with our spirituality.

This is the great new agenda of the church in our age. It is the prophetic role gay people of faith must play.

This story, the event of sexual/spiritual merger, signals the union of body and spirit. It opens the way to discussion of forbidden subjects in an atmosphere of open faith.

My experience was not unique. Thousands of other people have known similar experiences. Throughout history the message has been given. We have not been willing to talk about it.

Through our faith histories there has been a sexual and erotic component, often denied. Now it is coming forth as a healing agent. My story is our story. The freedom of gay sexuality has enabled the story to be told. Because we have so openly rebelled against the restricted structures of the past, we must tell the story.

Heterosexual people will hear the message. Perhaps they will resist at first. They will see the truth and confess their own experiences of sexual/spiritual merger. They, too, seek freedom and balance.

As we share these case histories, we create a new

body of knowledge and guide a new theology. Our lives and experiences write a new faith history. It is a uniquely homosexual history. We are the heralds of a new age. As bold or Messianic as that may sound, I believe it to be true. We have joined the great reformers of history, Luther, Calvin, Knox, John XXIII. We will renew the faith and bring new life to old traditions.

My star trilogy is just one small occurrence. It will elicit a multitude of other stories, as we begin to tell the truth about ourselves, our history, our faith, and our flesh.

The age of the merger of sex and spirit has begun. I invite the reader to add his or her story to my own.

V
Conclusion

What Have We Done?

We have named the sex negative factors which inhibit growth toward maturity and health for gays and non-gays. This effort is important. It begins to address the value system which no longer serves people's needs.

We have not thrown out tradition or Scripture. We have not abandoned the traditional family. We have expanded these social institutions and faith resources to include all people. Our efforts have been specifically directed toward the inclusion of homosexual persons within Western religious tradition.

Identifying the sex-negative social and religious heritage is just diagnostic. A physician must name the infectious agent; we have named the sex negative influences which form our tradition. To name the demon is to have power over it. Our process gives us power to move away from the fears and bondage of a negative structure and towards a positive and healthy lifestyle.

Gay people have brought together the spiritual and sexual in our lives. Here I have sought to define and demonstrate this healing process.

We have stopped being silent. We are now speaking out to name and claim the truth about ourselves and our faith. Silence is the great accomplice of ignorance. We have turned our attention to truth and knowledge through our speech. Gay Christian preachers are at the vanguard of a new morality. We preach a relevant truth which can restore integrity to old forms. Our witness is a voice crying in a wilderness filled with fear and legalisms.

Where Do We Go From Here?

Our task is to teach and preach the truth of our witness and reformation to every part of the church.

The future shall see our sex positive view of Scripture become the accepted and normative doctrine of the church. Gay clergy will serve openly in all churches. All churches will receive and acknowledge our gifts and faith.

Heterosexuals will be freed from the same negative and scripted roles we have been liberated from. Our freedom will be their freedom, but only after we have ceased to fear sexuality; only when we welcome truth.

I wish that this journey was an easy one. I expect the price of liberty to be high. No liberation is without martyrs. We have already seen gay leaders slain. We shall see more. Preachers and prophets will, no doubt, be our new martyrs. It is their message of sexual/

spiritual union which most threatens the established church.

I have seen too many families reject their gay children. This rejection often occurs when gay couples seek the church's blessing. Parents and others resist the merger of the sexual and the spiritual. Years of denial and resistance to sexual/spiritual union end when gay and lesbian couples symbolize their unions with religious rites.

Gay prophets must preach in gay churches, as well as non-gay churches. Councils and convocations of all denominations must be brought face to face with their gay and lesbian members. If they do not face them, they will have no spiritual vitality in the future.

By rejecting the gay clergy, the church has lost some of its most gifted leaders. The day is not far off when the denominations will ask us to come home and help them find their way. We can lead them out of their ignorance and fear. Mainline churches will need the expertise and experience of the gay clergy. They will want hopeful and relevant messages to offer future generations. Future generations will not take a sex negative religion seriously. Millions have already given up on the church as a viable institution. The gay religious movement is a part of an outreach to the vast unchurched community. We are bringing a new and positive vision to old traditions.

The homosexual clergy are not all serving the MCC or other predominantly gay congregations. The majority of gay clergy are in the established denominations. It is preposterous for a denomination to proclaim that they will not ordain homosexuals. They have ordained homosexuals throughout their history. Gay people have always been over-represented in the ministry and church leadership.

The Fall of the Kingdom of Fear

Great hope is found in this verse from Luke's Gospel: "For nothing is hid that shall not be made manifest, nor anything secret that shall not be known and come to light." (Luke 8:17 RSV).

When the lights go on everywhere, when the deeds and thoughts of all are revealed, it is going to be one great surprise after another.

It grieves me to hear religious leaders who are themselves homosexual pronounce condemnation upon gay people. Again and again I have seen gay people, closeted in fear, expose and condemn other gay people to protect themselves.

I have had occasion to work with powerful persons in government, notable religious leaders, as well as famous personalities. Some have confided to me their homosexual nature, yet denied it to the world. No amount of power, prestige, or money is worth lying about one's true nature. The energy required to maintain the pretense slowly destroys one's self-esteem. It feeds the sex negative system.

We can expect all closet doors to one day be opened. It is both tragic and ironic to think of how many homosexuals there will be among the "moral majority" and religious right wing. Religious systems built upon ignorance and fear will one day be exposed and topple. Countless numbers of gay men and women, who have hidden in their pious closets, will be revealed.

Religious zealots have used television and the media to spread their fearful message to gain profit and political power. Ultimately, the kingdom built on fear will fall. It cannot bear the light of truth. I cannot predict when this day will come. I can affirm my deep spiritual sense that it surely will come. My personal sorrow is that many gay men and lesbians will continue to suffer from the lies told by these religious zealots. They have given a bad name to millions of serious conservative Christians who seek justice, mercy, and love in their relationships.

The fall of the kingdom of fear will come, in part, when gay and lesbian prophets take to the airwaves to tell the truth about God, Gays, and the Gospel. Our story will shatter the fearful illusions of many. It will signal the end of ignorance and Biblical illiteracy.

Our message is not one of fear or hatred. No one need fear the coming age. It is built upon the truth that brings with it a sex positive, hopeful, and liberating force.

Our power rises to break the negative past. We will reveal a prosperity of spirit born of the merger of sexual and spiritual selves. This union is indeed holy.

Bibliographic Resources

England, Michael, *The Bible and Homosexuality*, Silver Spring, Maryland: UFMCC Department of Christan Social Action.

Boswell, John, *Christianity, Social Tolerance, and Homosexuality*, Chicago: University of Chicago Press. 1980.

McNeill, John J., S.J., *The Church and the Homosexual*, Kansas City: Sheed Andrews and McMeel Inc. 1976.

Mattison, Andrew, and McWhirter, David, *The Male Couple*, Englewood Cliff, New Jersey: Prentice Hall. 1984.

Mollenkott, Virginia, and Scanzoni, Letha, *Is the Homosexual My Neighbor?* New York: Harper and Row. 1978.

Uhrig, Larry J., *The Two of Us: Affirming, Celebrating, and Symbolizing Gay and Lesbian Relationships*, Boston: Alyson Publications. 1984.